IMAGES
of America

McDowell County

A MELTING POT OF NATIONS. Mary Kadar of Gary is shown here in her native Hungarian dance costume. Young people from Appalachian farms, African Americans from the South, and people from many Eastern European nations came to McDowell County in the late 1800s and early 1900s to make a better life for themselves and their families. Even though they were in a new land, they brought their traditions and heritage with them. (Courtesy of Patricia Kadar.)

IMAGES
of America

McDowell
County

William R. "Bill" Archer

ARCADIA
PUBLISHING

Published by Arcadia Publishing
Charleston, South Carolina

Library of Congress Catalog Card Number: 2005920916

For all general information contact Arcadia Publishing at:
Telephone 843-853-2070
Fax 843-853-0044
E-mail sales@arcadiapublishing.com
For customer service and orders:
Toll-Free 1-888-313-2665

Visit us on the Internet at www.arcadiapublishing.com

NO PLACE LIKE HOME. The Italian Camp at Adkins Branch, shown here in July 1902, dramatically demonstrates the housing challenges facing immigrants who came to McDowell County in search of jobs in the southern West Virginia coalfields. (Courtesy of Rose Marino.)

CONTENTS

ACKNOWLEDGMENTS

This is my third book in the Images of America series, and in many ways, it is one of the most challenging. McDowell County is one of the truly unique and special places on earth, and there is no way to do the county's heritage justice in one brief volume. However, my wife, Evonda Archer, and I have worked hard to gather images that share at least a part of the county's incredible story.

I owe a huge debt of thanks to many people who helped by supplying images for this work. Every image is special, and I wish to thank the following people for being part of this project by supplying photographs: H.C. "Kit" Lewis Jr., Robert Presley Jr., Patricia Kadar, Melvin Grubb, Nick Mason, Rose Marino, James Vaiden, Clyde Lambert, Sam Johnson, Ron Dalton, Carlton Viar, Sharon Walden, Bob Redd, Phil Farmer, Rev. Tim Hairston, Louise Warden, Mike Gianato, Henrietta White, Lindsay Grubb, the McDowell County Museum Commission, and the *Bluefield Daily Telegraph*.

Many others helped with the book in other supportive ways, including Al Hancock, Lori Hypes, Steve Gonzalez, and Ken Davidson, as well as Randy Deason, publisher of the *Bluefield Daily Telegraph*. The late Mike Hornick and the late Early Smith served as inspirations to me to explore McDowell County.

I dedicated my first book, *Bluefield*, to my friend Eddie Steele and my second book, *Mercer County*, to my mother, Florence V. Archer. I dedicate this book to my wife, Evonda—the love of my life.

INTRODUCTION

McDowell County, West Virginia, is more a state of mind than it is a geographical location. Tree-covered mountains roll from hollow to hollow, and from a distance, it seems hard to believe that people can survive in homes on hillsides as vertical as a cathedral steeple and in valleys where flash floods can emerge in a matter of moments without warning.

Some of America's most powerful and influential leaders in politics, military, business, industry, religion, and the arts have had either direct or indirect contact with McDowell County. In his famous "Notes on the State of Virginia," President Thomas Jefferson used information collected by Colonial explorer Dr. Thomas Walker to define what is now McDowell County as the "western country coal" lands. Walker's primary exploration in 1750 and Jefferson's "Notes" in 1781 attracted one of the nation's wealthiest investors, Robert Morris, often called the "financier of the American Revolution."

During the 1790s, Morris acquired huge tracts of land in western Virginia and Virginia's Kentucky Military District, with the largest of his personal holdings being the million-acre southern West Virginia coalfields, centered in McDowell County. Morris over-extended his financial resources by the end of the 1790s and was thrown into debtor's prison in 1798. He died in poverty and obscurity in 1806, and his massive holdings lay fallow.

In 1836, Prof. W.B. Rogers conducted a six-year survey of Virginia that further identified "the great western coal region." Rogers's 1836–1842 examination of Virginia—including an 1840 visit to McDowell County—spurred two individuals with unrelated backgrounds to play a role in what is today McDowell County. First, between 1847 and 1866, a Philadelphia cabinetmaker and veneer specialist, Michael Bouvier, became the front man for a group of investors who acquired about a half-million acres of Morris's southern West Virginia holdings. Michael Bouvier was the great uncle of Jacqueline Bouvier Kennedy Onassis.

The other, unrelated benefit of Rogers's survey was that a young eastern Pennsylvania adventurer, Jedediah Hotchkiss, got a taste of the profession and also an appreciation for the expanse of the coalfields. Hotchkiss would later work and teach in Staunton, Virginia. When the Civil War broke out, he worked as a civilian mapmaker for Gen. Thomas "Stonewall" Jackson. The war devastated Virginia, but Hotchkiss called on the state's leaders to abandon its agrarian past and embrace an industrial future.

In 1873, Hotchkiss sent Isaiah Arnold Welch to survey land held by the Maitland family, then owners of the 500,000-acre Wilson-Cary-Nichols grant previously owned by Morris and Bouvier. Hotchkiss extolled the steel-making virtues of coal from the Flat Top or Pocahontas

Coalfield through his Staunton-based newspaper, *The Virginias*. One of his readers was Samuel A. Crozer, a Chester, Pennsylvania entrepreneur with a successful Philadelphia-area rolling mill and Roanoke, Virginia iron furnace. Crozer convinced the Philadelphia-based investors who controlled the Norfolk & Western Railway (N&W) to tunnel through Coaldale Mountain to open up the McDowell County coalfields. The N&W built that tunnel in 1887, and within months, communities began to spring up along Elkhorn Creek, Browns Creek, and the Tug Fork of the Big Sandy River.

Crozer sent his vast profits back home to Upland, Pennsylvania, where the family invested in Upland Baptist Church, the Crozer-Chester Medical Center, several colleges, and the Crozer Theological Seminary—the school where Dr. Martin Luther King Jr. received his call to service in the civil rights movement.

Crozer was not alone in carving up the county and carting off the profits. Judge Elbert Gary, the architect of J.P. Morgan's U.S. Steel empire, acquired an enormous section of coal properties along the Tug Fork and produced the coking-coal to forge the steel for the industrialization of the United States. William M. Ritter built a timber empire out of McDowell's mountains, and a host of coal barons wrenched their fortunes from the county's rich mineral reserves.

McDowell County—the "Free State" as it is often called, possibly because no slaves lived there in the 1860 census—is more than just its industrial history. At its best, it represents the true melting pot of nations, where people of all colors, creeds, genders, and countries of origin can take part of the American dream. It is the state's "Cradle of Generals," home of champions, crucible of diversity, and birthplace of extraordinary beauty.

McDowell County is a geographical location, but her story is a story of people who, through adversity and against all odds, have achieved success without compromise and have triumphed in the face of incredible challenges.

Here, then, is the story of McDowell County.

One

COAL CAMP LIFE

BE IT EVER SO HUMBLE. The U.S. Coal and Coke Company, later known more commonly as its parent company, U.S. Steel Coal Mining, built housing for miners and their families who lived near the mine site, like the ones shown here at the No. 11 works between the present-day communities of Venus and Thorpe. (Courtesy of Grubb Photo Service.)

BRINGING CIVILIZATION TO THE WILDERNESS. In the mid-1880s, Samuel A. Crozer, a successful Philadelphia and Roanoke, Virginia businessman, acquired land in McDowell County to mine coal commercially and to fuel his Roanoke iron furnaces. After acquiring, through several agents including I.A. Welch and Thomas Graham, almost 8,000 acres of what is now known as Crozer Bottom along Elkhorn Creek, Crozer hired a fellow Pennsylvanian, John J. Lincoln, to develop his coal camp and mining operation. Lincoln was a devout Quaker driven by the spirit of industrialism that enveloped the nation in the late 19th and early 20th centuries. This

picture shows Lincoln's vision of a coal camp at Elkhorn. At the far left is the mining operation with various machine shops. Continuing from left to right, the Elkhorn Colored School stands on the hillside above a hotel-style temporary residence, with a residence for the family of a key company executive next door to the Lincoln residence. The central and far right section of the photo shows the Lincoln residence complete with darkly painted battens on the dormers. To the left of the Lincoln residence is a one-room schoolhouse built exclusively for the use of the three Lincoln children. To the right is the Lincoln family garden. (Courtesy of Rose Marino.)

HOW THE OTHER HALF LIVES. This picture of the business section of Lincoln's Elkhorn coal camp takes over where the previous photo left off. The Lincoln vegetable garden is at the far left, with the roof of the Elkhorn Post Office to the right of the garden. The wood-frame post office has a date of 1888 in its cornice and is still in use. The small cluster of homes to the right of the post office housed the community's families. While the residences of black and white coalminers were separated at the time—and for that matter, the white communities were separated by nation of origin—one black family, the Simpsons, lived in the housing near

the passenger station. Grant Simpson was Lincoln's personal barber, but he also operated a shop across from the passenger station. He maintained a small room in the back of the shop and employed another barber to cut hair for black customers. Simpson's oldest daughter, Elizabeth Simpson Drewry, gained fame in 1950 as the first black female elected to the West Virginia House of Delegates. The old Elkhorn School and company store are to the right of the passenger station, with housing for coalminers and their families visible at the right of the picture. (Courtesy of Rose Marino.)

GROWTH ON THE RIGHT TRACKS. The town of Davy, shown in this 1938 photo, grew along the N&W Railway tracks. (Courtesy of Louise Warden.)

WAITING FOR A TRAIN. A group of ninth-grade students from Anawalt School are shown here observing "Tacky Day" at the Anawalt Train Depot. From left to right are James Cochran, Andy Raisovitch, Jerry Moore, Alma "Peachie" Lafon, Reda Rhodes, Edna Brooks, Gloria Moore, Ruby Presley, Patty Music, Selma Sadler, Arletta Sadler, ? Whitehead, and Nancy Tabor. (Courtesy of Robert Presley Jr.)

WHAT A FRIEND. Religion has always played an important role in the life of the people of McDowell County. The congregation of the Pentecostal Holiness Church in Leckie is shown in this 1952 photograph. (Courtesy of Robert Presley Jr.)

A TRIP UP THE HOLLOW. The Ashland coal camp in Northfork Hollow was a hubbub of activity during the 1930s and stayed that way through several generations. Although the town itself remains rather dormant, the area has witnessed a resurgence of activity in the late 1990s and early 21st century with the popularity of four-wheelers. A plan is now in the offing to erect a campground in Ashland, restore the old company store to its mid-1930s splendor, and connect the area with the Hatfield-McCoy Trail System, a popular route for ATV riders. (Courtesy of Robert Presley Jr.)

ON THE STREET WHERE YOU LIVE. Main Street Crumpler was a bustling site in the early years of the 20th century. Crumpler is another Northfork Hollow coal camp that has seen an increase of activity as a result of the popularity of four-wheeling on ATVs. (Courtesy of Grubb Photo Service.)

BUSY BOTTOM. The Hemphill community was filled with homes and businesses during its heyday in the mid-20th century. Although many of the buildings are gone, the old Hemphill School has a new purpose. It is now a transitional housing unit for victims of domestic violence in a program developed by SAFE (Stop Abusive Family Environments). (Courtesy of Robert Presley Jr.)

GOOD TIMES IN MARYTOWN. The west-central Marytown coal camp started out strong, but received an infusion of capital *c.* 1920, when American automaker Henry Ford acquired the coalmine with the thought of manufacturing his own coke and steel to build his automobiles. When beset by problems of coal car availability and freight rates, Ford was reputed to have explored the idea of building a rail line to serve his Detroit-based businesses. That plan never materialized, and in a short time, Ford exited the coal business as well. (Courtesy of Robert Presley Jr.)

1937 Ford Ambulance
U.S. Coal & Coke Company
Gary, West Virginia
1937

READY TO ROLL. Even though Henry Ford's McDowell County dream was short lived, his products, like the 1937 ambulance shown here that served U.S. Coal and Coke Company coalminers, represented a reality for coalminers and their families in need of medical attention. (Courtesy of Robert Presley Jr.)

CLUBHOUSE TURN. The huge Main Gary Club House served single coalminers or miners whose families had not yet arrived in the coalfields. U.S. Coal and Coke Company operated other clubhouses for surrounding coal camps. The entire Gary concept was the brainchild of Judge Elbert Gary, architect of J.P. Morgan's U.S. Steel empire. (Courtesy of Grubb Photo Service.)

MAIN GARY WINTER SCENE. Judge Elbert Gary located his model coal camp in a big bend of the Tug Fork of the Big Sandy River. Among the first structures to appear were the passenger station, a restaurant, and a company store, as shown in this photo from the early 1900s. (Courtesy of Robert Presley Jr.)

19

BY THE OLD MILL STREAM. Mill Creek Coal and Coke was owned by John Cooper and had operations on both sides of Coaldale Mountain. While the McDowell County operation was also called the Coaldale Mine, both operations worked under the banner of the same parent company, Mill Creek. The Mercer County side operation in Coopers was opened in 1884. (Courtesy of Grubb Photo Service.)

PLAY BALL. Gridiron action fostered intense rivalries throughout the coalfields. The field shown here was located near the Union Supply Company store near Venus, Gary No. 10, U.S. Coal and Coke works. (Courtesy of Grubb Photo Service.)

MODERN DEVELOPMENT. U.S. Coal and Coke's Elbert coal camp featured modern homes for coalminers and their families, even though they were light on insulation according to some families who resided there. (Courtesy of Grubb Photo Service.)

PAY DAY. Coalminers and their families came to the Pocahontas Fuel Company scrip office in Jenkinjones to pick up their earnings, less the deductions withheld by the company for housing, food, clothes, tools, and other items. Coal companies paid miners in "scrip," coins and paper money manufactured by the company that could be used only for goods and services provided by the company. Paris Johnson Bailey is seated above. (Courtesy of Paul L. Bailey.)

GARY DISTRICT. The big building shown in the middle of the above photo, Gary District High School, served African-American students of families that lived and worked in the U.S. Coal and Coke mines. The smaller building in front of the school was a restaurant and barbershop for black families in the area. (Courtesy of Bob Redd.)

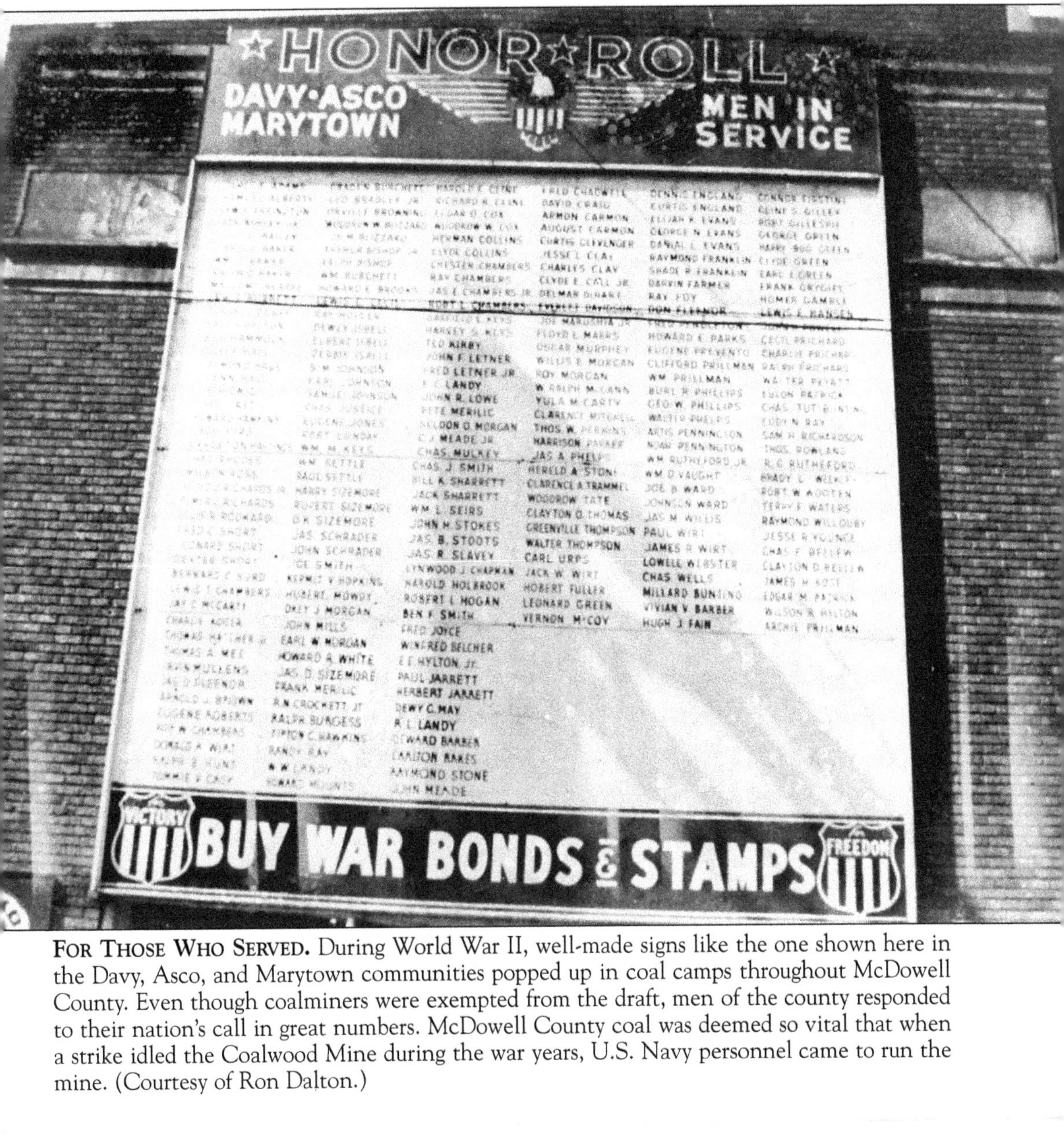

FOR THOSE WHO SERVED. During World War II, well-made signs like the one shown here in the Davy, Asco, and Marytown communities popped up in coal camps throughout McDowell County. Even though coalminers were exempted from the draft, men of the county responded to their nation's call in great numbers. McDowell County coal was deemed so vital that when a strike idled the Coalwood Mine during the war years, U.S. Navy personnel came to run the mine. (Courtesy of Ron Dalton.)

HIGH WATER. Bringing 20th-century infrastructure to McDowell County proved challenging both mentally and physically, as this Elkhorn Valley water tower attests. Although many coal camps had indoor water service, only a few sewage-treatment facilities existed in the county early on. Many coal communities continue to struggle without sewage treatment plants and with an aging public water infrastructure. (Courtesy of H.C. "Kit" Lewis Jr.)

NEITHER RAIN NOR SLEET.
Because of the geographical
separation of many McDowell coal
camps, U.S. Post Office clerks sorted
mail on the mail train as it moved
from community to community
through McDowell County.
(Courtesy of James Vaiden.)

THE MAIL MUST GO THROUGH.
According to James Vaiden, who
at 80 still works at the Welch Post
Office, about 200 passenger trains
converged on Cincinnati, Ohio,
daily. Vaiden's first experience on
the mail train was during Christmas
1945, on the run between Welch
and Jenkinjones. (Courtesy of
James Vaiden.)

BANK BUSINESS. The coal industry brought wealth to McDowell County, and banks like the First National Bank of Anawalt sprang up to serve coal companies, coalminers, and their families. According to local historian Robert Presley Jr., the Bank of Anawalt fell victim to the Great Depression in the 1930s. (Courtesy of Robert Presley Jr.)

EARLY TIMES. The Gary story started with a wink and a nod in 1901, but the town of Gary had grown significantly by the time of this 1908 photograph. Judge Elbert H. Gary, working with Bramwell banker Isaac T. Mann, bought 230,000 acres of Tug Fork coal property for $10 million. Gary and Mann also bought an additional 70,000 acres from W.M. Ritter and W.G.W. Iaeger for $3.5 million. The N&W Railway re-purchased all 300,000 acres from Gary for $20 million and leased 20,000 acres back to him on December 31, 1901. (Courtesy of Robert Mills.)

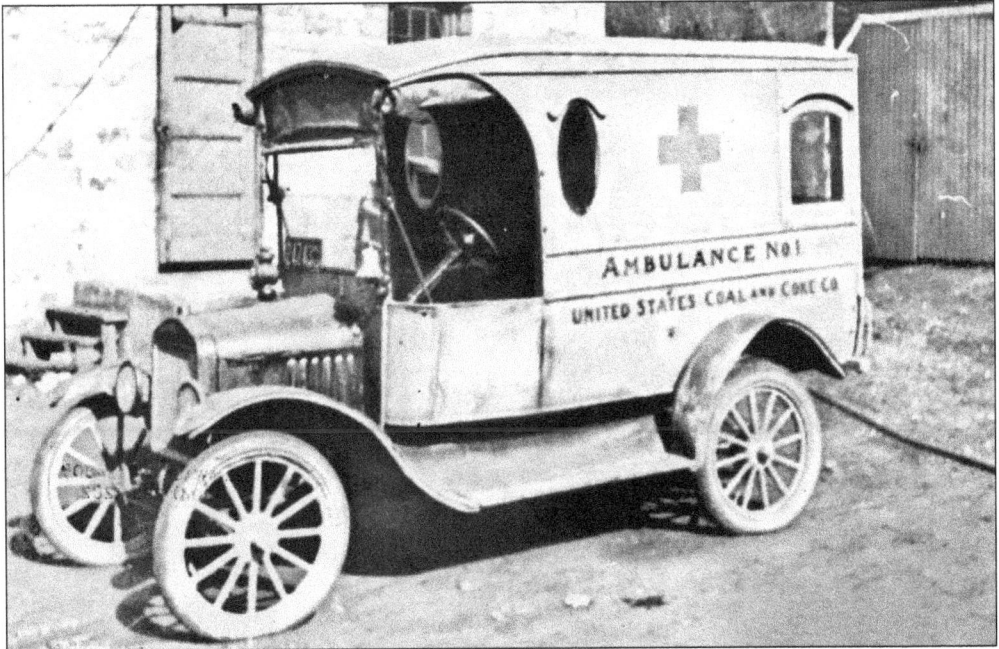

EMERGENCY RESPONDERS. Early ambulances, like the one shown here in 1920, served injured U.S. Coal and Coke coalminers. The U.S. Steel mines enjoyed a great safety record during their 80-year-plus run in Gary Hollow. (Courtesy of Robert Presley Jr.)

LET'S DANCE. McDowell County truly represented a "melting pot of nations," with cultural heritage from many countries becoming a part of everyday life in the coalfields. A Hungarian dance class is shown at the Gary American Red Cross hall, c. 1925. (Courtesy of Patricia Kadar.)

SCENE OF TRAGEDY. An explosion at the Bottom Creek Mine on November 18, 1911, killed 14 coalminers and 4 engineers who were inspecting mined-out "rooms" at the time of the explosion. The mine was located between Keystone and Kimball. (Courtesy of Grubb Photo Service.)

TOWN UNDER CONSTRUCTION. The Elbert community, named for Judge Elbert Gary, is shown here in No. 7 Bottom. The large building in the foreground is the company store/theater complex. (Courtesy of Grubb Photo Service.)

SHOP FOR BARGAINS. The Pocahontas Collieries store in Jenkinjones, *c.* 1925–1930, was a formidable structure in the remote coal-mining community. (Courtesy of Grubb Photo Service.)

INSIDE JOB. Pocahontas Fuel Co. store personnel in Jenkinjones, also *c.* 1925–1930, are, from left to right, ? Sayers, Elwood Bailey, Red Bailey, and P.J. Bailey. (Courtesy of Grubb Photo and Robert Presley Jr.)

TEE HE. Veteran U.S. Steel retiree Jim Spencer is shown teeing off at the former Gary Country Club, now called the Black Wolf Links, in Skygusty. (Photo by the author.)

UPHILL BATTLE. The seventh green at the old Gary Country Club course features a steep climb and bunkers straight out of the early 1920s. U.S. Steel built the course so its young executives could have a place to enjoy outdoor recreation. (Photo by the author.)

PLAY BALL. Baseball has always been a big attraction in the southern West Virginia coalfields, as this early 20th-century photo of a game in Keystone will attest. Some area residents think the large tent may indicate the presence of a religious gathering. Rev. Billy Sunday traveled through the region converting souls at about this time. (Courtesy of H.C. "Kit" Lewis Jr.)

Two

OLD TIMES

HORSING AROUND. At least 17 mule teams are shown here working to carve out a channel and level a portion of the Tug Fork of the Big Sandy River at this unknown location near the turn of the 20th century. (Courtesy of Grubb Photo Service.)

COURTING. The first session of the McDowell County circuit court was held on August 23, 1858, at the home of George W. Payne in Perryville (today's town of English). The first courthouse, shown above, was located in the Wilco section of Gary. (Courtesy of Robert Presley Jr.)

COMMISSIONERS. McDowell County's second courthouse, shown above c. 1901, was located on Shannon Branch in what later became Gary No. 1. (Courtesy of Robert Presley Jr.)

VOTE EARLY AND OFTEN. Two McDowell County natives and math whiz kids determined the time, date, and location of this photograph, completely unidentified except that it was matted by "Brown Brothers, Keystone." Roger "Red" Barnett and Davis Woolum determined—based on the shadows, the clock, and a number of complex computations—that the picture was taken on Main Street in Keystone at 12:40 p.m. on Election Day, November 2, 1912. Woolum now lives in Bluefield, Virginia, and Barnett lives in Florida, but they both played baseball at Iaeger High School in the late 1940s. (Courtesy of H.C. "Kit" Lewis Jr.)

DAPPER DAY. This photograph of a gentleman driving along an old dirt road was among a group of photographs taken in the Keystone-Northfork area, although neither the gentleman nor the location is identified. (Courtesy of H.C. "Kit" Lewis Jr.)

BRIDGE TO THE FUTURE. The photograph of this bridge construction scene was likely taken somewhere along Elkhorn Creek. The actual location is unknown. (Courtesy of H.C. "Kit" Lewis Jr.)

36

FLOOD DAMAGE. The bridge shown here at the Elkridge Section of Keystone, crossing the North Fork of Elkhorn Creek, appears to have been damaged in one of the frequent flash floods that continue to ravage the area. (Courtesy of H.C. "Kit" Lewis Jr.)

MORE FLOODING. Elkhorn Creek is shown here at Keystone after an early 20th-century flood. A.L. Calhoun's restaurant and bar was a popular spot during the early decades of the century. Calhoun and Dr. G.T. Epling, one-time mayor of Keystone, were supposedly the joint political bosses of Keystone c. 1912. (Courtesy of H.C. "Kit" Lewis Jr.)

BEFORE RAIL. Few roads and rugged mountainous terrain served as a bane to travel in McDowell County before the railroad became well established. McDowell County teamsters, like the ones shown here at an unknown location, were equal to the task. (Courtesy of H.C. "Kit" Lewis Jr.)

GREAT DAY IN HEALTHCARE. Workers and dignitaries posed for this 1900 photo of groundbreaking on Welch Miners Hospital No. 1, now Welch Community Hospital. Dr. Henry D. Hatfield was elected president of the hospital board on August 8, 1901. Hatfield, a Republican, was elected governor of West Virginia in 1912.

TOWN NAMED FOR A STATE NICKNAME. The City of Keystone, founded in 1893, was named after Pennsylvania's nickname, "The Keystone State," earned during the American Revolution because of its position in the middle of the original 13 colonies. James B. Stephenson was president of the mine, and J.F.K. Steele was secretary/treasurer and mine superintendent. Keystone had an infamous reputation among southern West Virginia towns, primarily because of the city's notorious red-light district, called "Cinder Bottom." Keystone made national headlines on July 4, 1910, as a result of a fracas that erupted after the Johnson-Jeffries heavyweight championship fight, and again on September 1, 1999, when the Officer of the Comptroller of the Currency declared the First National Bank of Keystone insolvent, closed the bank, and appointed the Federal Deposit Insurance Corporation (FDIC) receiver of the failed bank's $1.1 billion in assets. (Courtesy of H.C. "Kit" Lewis Jr.)

WE'LL BE TRAVELING SOON. Mr. and Mrs. John Calloway are shown here waiting to catch a train bound for their honeymoon at an undisclosed location. The Calloways are the grandparents of Mildred Martha Via of Northfork. (Courtesy of Mildred Martha Via.)

TUG VALLEY HOME. The board-and-batten structure shown here is one of the early homes of the Anawalt area. (Courtesy of Robert Presley Jr.)

I COULD WRITE A SONNET. Dr. L.L. Whitney and his wife, Elizabeth, are shown in their horse-drawn carriage outside the family's Eckman home in 1917. (Courtesy of Patricia Kadar.)

WORKING IN A COAL MINE. Two coalminers are shown here headed underground in one of the U.S. Coal and Coke Company mines in Gary Hollow, sometime in the days before safety standards related to protective headgear and other safety measures. (Courtesy of H.C. "Kit" Lewis Jr.)

HAPPY HOLIDAYS. The snow-covered sidewalks of Main Gary do not appear to present a major challenge to travelers on a winter day. (Courtesy of Patricia Kadar.)

NEED A LIFT? Frank Hunt is shown here at his taxi stand in Main Gary. Hunt was born in Anawalt in 1906. (Courtesy of Patricia Kadar.)

WELL TRAINED. Five men are shown here posing for this 1904 photograph, standing in front of the old Keystone N&W Railway station. Among the men shown here are J.M. Bell, T.W. King, agent A.F. Hudson, and a man known as Uncle Jake. (Courtesy of Robert Presley Jr.)

Three

RAIL AND COAL

LIVING THE GOOD LIFE. Passengers of the ultra-modern *Powhatan Arrow* cruised through McDowell County in the lap of luxury. Actually, the people shown here are models posing for several photos that accompanied the press kits distributed to 52 press and radio people who actually traveled on the *Arrow*'s first run, on April 28, 1946. (Courtesy of Carlton Viar.)

A J-CLASS OF ITS OWN. The Norfolk Southern J-Class steam locomotives were state of the art in post–World War II steam-powered locomotives. The J-611 is shown here on a "drive by" at Kimball during a steam excursion from Bluefield to Iaeger in 1989. The 611 is on permanent display at the Transportation Museum in Roanoke, Virginia. (Photo from the *Bluefield Daily Telegraph* archives.)

ART OF TRAVEL. Models are shown here demonstrating the comfortable club car on the *Powhatan Arrow*. In later years, the westbound *Arrow* was designated the "Pocahontas." The *Arrow* made steady runs between Norfolk and Cincinnati. (Courtesy of Carlton Viar.)

DIVERSE WORKFORCE. Workers of the Algoma Coal tipple crew are shown here ready for their shift. The diversity of McDowell County's workforce was one of its greatest strengths. Randall Wright provided the names of the men shown here. They are, from left to right, (front row) Bill Davis, John W. "Jack" Wright, and Otis Pennington; (back row) Bury "Toke" Thomas, Junior Green, Maynard Pike, Theodore Hale, Hamp Glover, and Herbert Hale. (Courtesy of Grubb Photo Service.)

PIONEERS OF THE FLAT TOP COALFIELD. Several early coal barons posed for this early 20th-century photo in front of the wooden trestle near Jenkinjones. Jenkin Jones, the man for whom the town is named, is seated second from the left. (Courtesy of Grubb Photo Service.)

DRAINWAY CREW. Workers posed for this June 13, 1938 photograph in Boissevain, Virginia, after completing an 18.6-mile-long underground drainage system that carried water from the Boissevain and Pocahontas mines in Virginia and the Jenkinjones, Amonate, and Bishop mines in McDowell County. (Courtesy of Grubb Photo Service.)

48

MOTOR DRIVER. Coalminers are shown here exiting the driftmouth (mine entry at the exposed coal seam) of the Tug Mine in Anawalt. (Courtesy of Grubb Photo Service.)

MOTOR ADVANCEMENTS. A motor operator is shown here bringing a motor out of the driftmouth of Koppers Coal Company's Keystone mine. (Courtesy of Grubb Photo Service.)

THE LITTLE ENGINE THAT COULD. A Norfolk & Western steam locomotive is shown here bobtailing across the N&W trestle in Maybeury in this photo dated February 28, 1948. (From the author's collection.)

TRAIN WRECK. One of the region's worst train wrecks took place June 30, 1937, when a westbound time freight locomotive and 45 cars left the tracks in Maybeury and plunged 180 feet, killing the engineer, fireman, a brakeman, and a child at the crash site. (Courtesy of Grubb Photo Service.)

BOILER EXPLODES. When Train No. 85 landed beneath the Maybeury trestle, the boiler exploded and flew 893 feet from the scene of the 1937 train wreck. Although U.S. Route 52 was closed for several days, curiosity seekers from a wide area came to observe the tremendous wreck. Among the many stories that followed the wreck was one that old-timers recalled of another wreck at the same location on December 5, 1893. (Courtesy of Grubb Photo Service.)

READY FOR WORK. Miners on the day shift of the Vera Pocahontas No. 3 Mine in Landgraff posed for this July 9, 1940 photograph. Clyde Lambert (third row, fourth from left) was visiting an establishment many years after the picture was taken, when the proprietor said that if anyone in the place was in the picture, they could have it. (Courtesy of Clyde Lambert.)

DAY SHIFT AT LANDGRAFF. Both halves of the above photograph represent a clear view of the diversity of the McDowell County workforce. African-American coalminers from the South worked shoulder-to-shoulder with coalminers from several Eastern European countries to mine coal to fuel the nation's industrial revolution. (Courtesy of Clyde Lambert.)

BONE PICKERS. During the hand-loading days of coal mining, coalminers removed impurities from coal, graded it by size, and placed it on the appropriate conveyor belt for loading, as this Underwood and Underwood of Washington, D.C. photograph clearly shows. The men working here are shown at the Pocahontas Fuel Company Norfolk-Angle Tipple in Maybeury. (Courtesy of Robert Presley Jr.)

MAKING A HEAD OF STEAM. A Norfolk & Western steam locomotive is shown here making steam in the N&W yard in Iaeger. (Courtesy of Robert Presley Jr.)

LAYING TRACK. A crew is shown here laying track at Millcreek Coal's Elkhorn Mine near Maybeury in the 1930s. (Courtesy of Grubb Photo Service.)

STICKING TO THE UNION. The United Mine Workers of America are shown here at a gathering in Welch in 1921. Famous union activist Mother Jones is shown in the middle of this photo from the West Virginia Historical Archives. Some historians date the start of the West Virginia Mine Wars from August 1, 1921, when Matewan sheriff Sid Hatfield and Ed Chambers were killed at the McDowell County Courthouse in Welch. (Courtesy of Robert Presley Jr.)

SOLEMN SENTINEL. In recent years, the families of coalminers who have passed away erected this coalminers' monument in Bradshaw, near McDowell's western border with Buchanan County, Virginia. The January 10, 1940 explosion at the Bartley Mine was the county's deadliest disaster, killing 91 coalminers. (Photo by the author.)

ICE COLD COKE. The coke ovens at U.S. Coal and Coke's No. 8 works in Elbert were in use through the late 19th and early 20th centuries. Coke is the product that remains after the impurities have been burned off coal. It is used in the steel-making process. (Courtesy of Patricia Kadar.)

FROM THE INSIDE OUT. The old beehive coke ovens lit up the McDowell County countryside during the early 20th century, but they are now little more than relics of the past, as one can tell in this view from inside a Filbert coke oven. (Photo by Evonda Archer.)

SMOKESTACK INDUSTRY. The old smokestack at the Eastern Gas and Fuel Carswell prep plant is barely visible in this 1936 photograph. (Courtesy of Grubb Photo Service.)

LOAD OUT. Coal cars are shown here in 1970 being loaded at the Hawley Coal Mining prep plant near Keystone. (Courtesy of Grubb Photo Service.)

MINE DISASTER SITE. This scene at the Jed Coal and Coke Company Mine near Havaco was taken after a March 26, 1912 explosion claimed the lives of 83 coalminers. The coalminers killed in the explosion were buried near the mine at a location called Little Egypt. The graves were never moved, but after the temporary markers disappeared, later generations of residents used the graveyard as a garden. (Courtesy of Grubb Photo Service.)

DIFFERENT NAME. After World War II, a different coal company reopened the Jed Mine under a new name—the Havaco Mine. On January 15, 1946, an explosion at Havaco killed 15 coalminers. Other mine tragedies include: September 15, 1902, Algoma, 17 dead; February 23, 1905, Wilco, 7 dead; July 5, 1905, Vivian, 5 dead; November 4, 1905, Vivian, 7 dead; January 4, 1906, Coaldale, 22 dead; December 29, 1908, Lick Branch, 50 dead; January 12, 1909, Lick Branch, 67 dead; November 18, 1911, Bottom Creek, 18 dead; December 15, 1917, Yukon, 18 dead; July 18, 1918, Craswell, 6 dead; March 25, 1924, Yukon, 24 dead; May 13, 1927, Caples, 8 dead; April 2, 1928, Keystone, 5 dead; May 22, 1928, Yukon, 17 dead; November 30, 1928, Roderfield, 6 dead; January 22, 1941, Carswell, 5 dead; August 6, 1948, Caples, 5 dead; February 4, 1957, Bishop, 37 dead; December 27, 1957, Amonate, 11 dead; October 27, 1958, Bishop, 22 dead; and September 25, 1964, Bradshaw, 3 dead. (Courtesy of Robert Presley Jr.)

CUSTOM BLEND. U.S. Steel's Alpheus preparation plant was state of the art in blending a variety of coals from Gary's different "works" on the Tug Fork. The plant was shut down in the mid-1980s after U.S. Steel opened its No. 50 Pinnacle Mine on the Welch-Pineville Road. (Courtesy of Grubb Photo Service.)

SAFETY FIRST. U.S. Coal and Coke's "safety board," pictured in 1924, indicated when any of the company's 11 coalmines, the power plant, or the shop had a work stoppage because of an on-the-job injury. The company earned a long-standing reputation for safety underground. (Courtesy of Robert Presley Jr.)

WAR YEARS. The Central Pocahontas Coal Company mine at Caples was a big coal producer during its heyday, as can be seen in this 1944 photograph. In recent years, the Caples area has been in the news as a proposed location for a new landfill. (Courtesy of Grubb Photo Service.)

COALWOOD'S TWIN. The Caretta Mine represented the second component of the Coalwood-Caretta mining complex. (Courtesy of Grubb Photo Service.)

REMOTE OPERATION. Pond Creek Pocahontas Coal's Raysal operation was located in a remote part of the county, near the border with Buchanan County, Virginia. (Courtesy of Grubb Photo Service.)

SAME HOLLOW. Pond Creek Pocahontas Coal's No. 6 processing plant in Bradshaw was also located in a remote location, but with the improvement of roads, coalminers did not have to live at the mine, as may be seen in this 1955 photograph. (Courtesy of Robert Presley Jr.)

HOME OF THE ROCKET BOYS. Olga Coal Company's No. 1 tipple in Coalwood is shown in this 1936 photograph. Homer Hickam Sr. would later serve as superintendent of the mine. His son, Homer Hickam Jr., brought great fame to the region with his memoirs, *Rocket Boys*, which was later made into the movie *October Sky*. (Courtesy of Robert Presley Jr.)

BIG OPERATION. The Keystone mining complex, including the mine and preparation plant, has been in continuous operation at essentially the same location for more than a century. In 2005, the prep plant remains active, processing coal from several other mines in the area. (Courtesy of Grubb Photo Service.)

THE MEN OF ELKHORN. Day-shift coalminers of Crozer Coal and Coke Company's No. 4 Mine posed for this photograph on June 10, 1940. The Crozer family played a significant role in the early stages of America's Industrial Revolution, bringing British power-weaving technology to textile plants they established in the Philadelphia area. After the start of the Civil War, the federal government acquired a normal school Crozer established in Chester and transformed it into a large hospital for Union soldiers. Following the Battle of Gettysburg, the hospital treated wounded soldiers of both sides. Among the wounded Confederates treated at the hospital was David E. Johnston, who would later become a well-known author, lawyer, judge, and businessman. A new breed of leadership emerged after the war to resurrect

Virginia's economy on an industrial model. Jed Hotchkiss of Staunton, Virginia, pushed for the development of McDowell County's coalfields through his trade publication, *The Virginias*. Hotchkiss hired Isaiah A. Welch to survey the coalfield. After Philadelphia investors acquired the old Atlantic, Mississippi, and Ohio Railroad and transformed it into the Norfolk & Western in 1882, Hotchkiss set about attracting investors. Samuel A. Crozer provided help to the Southwest Virginia Improvement Company following an 1884 mine explosion at Pocahontas, Virginia. Three years later, Welch, Thomas Graham, David French, and David Johnston were in McDowell County acquiring the property that would become Crozer Bottom. (Courtesy of Ron Dalton.)

MEN AND TIMBERS. Paul Underwood (foreground) and other coalminers are shown leaving the Red Robin Coal Company mine at Premier Mountain in this July 1940 photograph. Timber harvested in the region had many usages underground, ranging from roof supports to brattice works. (Courtesy of Grubb Photo Service.)

PRIMO. The Premier Pocahontas Collieries Company mine at the base of Premier Mountain was one of the major coal operations along U.S. Route 52, west of Welch. A U.S. Army Air Corps transport plane crashed near here on July 1, 1942, killing all aboard. The local VFW post maintains a monument to the memory of those who perished in the accident. (Courtesy of Grubb Photo Service.)

UNDER CONSTRUCTION. The photo here shows a crew working to build the Norfolk & Western Railway Station in Berwind in 1906. Only a few of the old board-and-batten buildings that once dotted the countryside remain. The old N&W Station at War serves as town hall. (Courtesy of Robert Presley Jr.)

ON THE ELKHORN CREEK SIDE. The old Barlow tipple, just outside Maybeury, was among the early tipples built during the hand-loading days of the McDowell County coalfields. (Courtesy of Grubb Photo Service.)

WITHOUT PEER. The old Peerless Coal Company operation shown in this photograph demonstrates both the need to have employees near the prep plant as well as the late-1950s trend toward coalminers who lived elsewhere and commuted to the mine site. McDowell's population neared 100,000 people in 1950 but has declined to less than a fourth of that total in 50 years. (Courtesy of Grubb Photo Service.)

MOUNTAINSIDE PREP PLANT. The old Jenkinjones tipple and prep plant is distinctive in the McDowell coalfields, at least in part because of the massive stone retaining wall that provided a stable foundation for the mine from the late 19th century until the mid-1980s. (Photo by Melvin Grubb.)

Four

PERSONALITIES

MCDOWELL PEOPLE SHAPE THE COUNTY. People associated with the old McNary and Johnson Company Hardware Store in Welch posed for this early photograph. According to a 1907 directory of the coalfields, a man named J.F. Johnson Jr. operated a department store in Welch, but the directory does not include information about the hardware store. (Courtesy of Rose Marino.)

McDowell Royalty. Screen legend Douglas Fairbanks Jr. and his wife, Keystone native Mary Lee Epling-Fairbanks, are shown here with their daughter, Daphne Fairbanks-Kay. The marriage marked the second union for each person. Fairbanks had been married to Joan Crawford of *Mommy Dearest* fame and Epling-Fairbanks had been married to A&P heir Huntington Hartford, whom she met while attending finishing school in Boston. The two met on New Year's Day 1939 and married April 22, 1939, after a brief courtship. The Fairbanks' had three daughters: Daphne, Melissa Morant, and Victoria Fairbanks. Mrs. Fairbanks died of cancer on September 14, 1988. Her father was Keystone dentist Giles Thomas Epling, and her mother was Nancy Agness White Epling, a member of a bedrock Mercer County family that lived in the Oakvale area. (Courtesy of Henrietta White.)

PERFECT POSE. P.P. "Posey" Belcher is shown here posing with a photograph of the McDowell County Centennial king and queen. Belcher was an official with Bluefield Hardware who lived in Northfork and operated a hardware store. The major event of the 1958 centennial was the performance of *Our Changing Hills: A Story of McDowell County*, staged at Maroon Wave Stadium May 12–17, 1958. (Courtesy of Northfork mayor Nick Mason.)

COAL CHAMPION. The one individual who was most well known for his role in aiding the plight of downtrodden coalminers was John L. Lewis, who served as president of the United Mine Workers of America from 1920 until his retirement in 1960. Although he was a native of Lucas, Iowa, Lewis was revered by coalminers and their families throughout McDowell County and the coalfields. Lewis led the fight to organize the southern coalfields against stiff opposition from coal operators. McDowell County was a key battleground location in that struggle. (Courtesy of Louise Warden.)

BIRTH OF AN INDUSTRY. This photo shows a group of coalminers who lived at Little Creek, near Anawalt, in 1884. Seated are G.W. Sadler (left) and Joe Lambert (right). Standing, from left to right, are O.P. Bailey, A.H. Lambert, and Harvey Bailey. Mining operations active in 1884 included the Pocahontas Mine on the Virginia side and the Mill Creek Coal and Coke Mine in Mercer County. The McDowell fields did not open until 1887–1888. (Courtesy of Robert Presley Jr.)

A RACE FOR ALL TIME. Scores of stories abound surrounding presidential candidate John F. Kennedy's 1960 campaign swings through southern West Virginia. This photo shows Kennedy holding a very young Mike Gianato as his proud father, Mike Gianato Sr., looks on. Kennedy worked the coalfields for every vote in both the 1960 Democratic primary and the general election. According to Mike Gianato Sr., after this photo appeared in *Look* magazine, he wrote the publication to get his own copy—a copy that now hangs in Gianato's Grocery Store in Kimball, where the photo was taken. (Courtesy of Mike Gianato Sr.)

TYPE CASTING. Students of the Gary High School typing class are shown mastering their lessons in this 1946 photograph. McDowell County students were well prepared to enter any business or profession. Patricia Hunt (Kadar) is the last student in the back row. (Courtesy of Patricia Kadar.)

GARY FRESHMAN CLASS, 1944. Students of the Gary High School (GHS) freshman class of 1944 are shown here. African-American students of the communities served by GHS attended Gary District High School. The GHS athletic teams were known as the Coal Diggers, and the Gary District teams were the Bulldogs. (Courtesy of Patricia Kadar.)

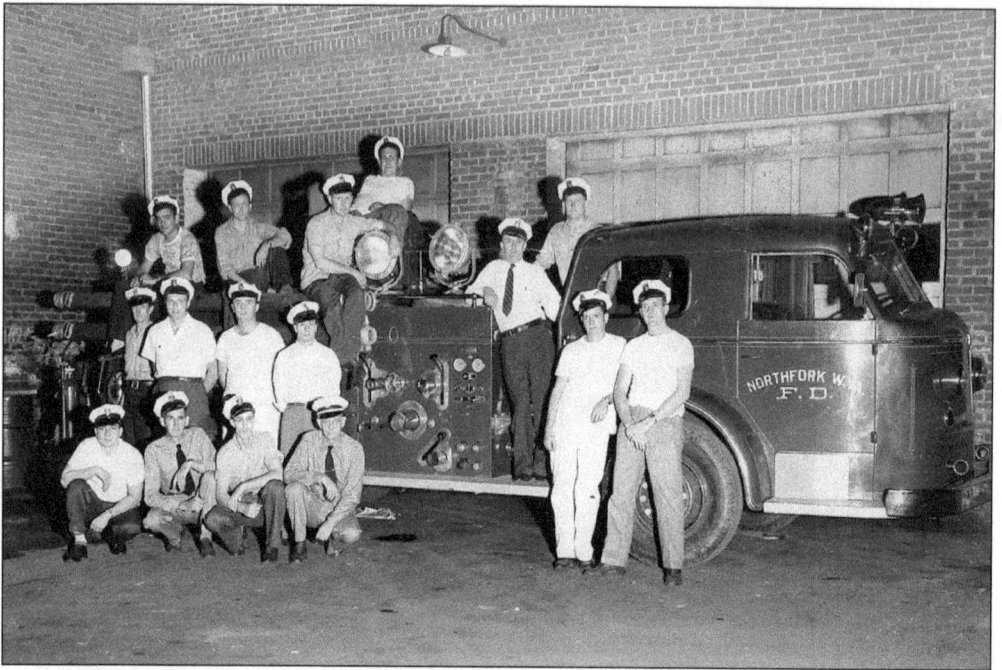

FIREFIGHTERS. Members of the Northfork Fire Department shown in this 1949 photograph include, in no specific order, Fred Gint, Clyde Johnson, Mack Herndon, Mike Brown, Walter Jones, Pete Angelelli, Worth Norris, Frank Otey, Bill Hale, Bill Miller, Saunders Thornton, Luther Collins, W.R. Merideth, and Stewart Mitchell. (Courtesy of Nick Mason.)

BAND AID. The Elkhorn-Northfork Junior High School Band is shown here after Elkhorn and Northfork were combined following integration. Litz Armbrister served as band director. (Courtesy of Nick Mason.)

AFL GLORY DAYS. Gordon "Pig" Lambert, a Pageton native, played a stint with the Denver Broncos of the old American Football League, back in the days before the leagues were merged. Lambert is just one of many McDowell natives who made a mark in the professional athletic ranks. For the last several years, Lambert has been active in McDowell County politics and currently serves as president of the county commission. (Courtesy of Gordon Lambert.)

A CAREER OF SERVICE. Elizabeth Simpson Drewry was the first black woman elected to the West Virginia House of Delegates, and she gained national acclaim for her unwavering honesty and refusal to participate in corrupt political practices of the past. She was born in Virginia, but her family moved to Elkhorn when she was very young. Her father, Grant Simpson, worked as a barber. Drewry worked as an educator in the county's black schools and became interested in politics. She was unsuccessful in her first run for the house, in a race that was contested in the courts, but in 1950 she won. During her first term, she refused to accept a bribe in exchange for her support of a coal industry vote, and the uproar that followed put her in the national spotlight. She served with distinction until 1964, when illness forced her to resign. She died September 24, 1979, and is buried somewhere in the all-black Oak Grove Cemetery near Bluefield. (Photo from the author's collection.)

MINORITY OPPORTUNITIES. The late Suzanne Slaughter stands in this 1923 photograph at 17, with her mother seated in the foreground. Slaughter was a gifted educator who served as principal at Eckman School prior to serving in other administrative positions with the school system after integration. Slaughter was an advocate of good education throughout her life, as well as one of the driving forces behind the restoration of the Kimball War Memorial. (From the author's collection.)

ROCKET MAN. Homer H. Hickam, shown here in this 1998 publicity photograph by John Earl, gained fame after publishing a memoir titled *Rocket Boys*, later made into a feature film titled *October Sky*. (From the Delacorte Press publicity packet.)

THE MAYOR. W.B. Swope served as mayor of Welch for several years and was instrumental in developing the Welch Co-Op, which keeps natural gas prices low for city residents. He died January 24, 2001, at age 85. (Photo by the author.)

PLAY BALL. Members of the 1951 Coalwood Robins baseball team are shown here. The team played in the old Coalfields League. The Robins were one of the four initial teams in the league that was formed in 1924 but folded the following year. The Olga Coal No. 1 Mine sponsored the Robins. (Courtesy of Cecil Surratt.)

PLAY (SOFT) BALL. Members of the 1950 Coalwood Soft Ball Championship team are, from left to right, R.L. Linkous (school principal), Dr. E.E. Hale (dentist), unidentified, Eugene Mauck (coal company superintendent), two unidentified coal company engineers, and Cecil Surratt. (Courtesy of Cecil Surratt.)

INFIELD FLY RULE. Cecil Surratt of the Coalwood Robins baseball team is posed here as though he is camped out under a fly ball. Surratt played second base for the Robins. (Courtesy of Cecil Surratt.)

POWER PLAY. Deacon Samuel Johnson, a one-time mayor of Keystone, is shown here during his glory days as center of the 1940–1941 Gary District Bulldogs. (Courtesy of Sam Johnson.)

FORT KNOX. J. Knox McConnell, former president of the First National Bank of Keystone, is shown in this 1987 photograph with unsuccessful Republican gubernatorial candidate and Morgantown businessman John Raese and unsuccessful Republican congressional candidate Maryann Brewster. McConnell served as finance chairman of President George Bush's campaign. (Photo by the author.)

KNOX'S FOXES. McConnell assembled a female-dominated staff at the First National Bank of Keystone. From left to right are Billie Jean Cherry, Vicki Mikels, Nancy Vorono, McConnell, Terry Lee Church, and Melissa Quizenbeury. Cherry and Church remain in federal prison after convictions on various fraud and obstruction charges, while Quizenbeury pleaded guilty to Security Exchange Commission fraud and has served her time. (Photo from the author's collection.)

83

CARE GIVERS. The staff of the Pocahontas Coal Company hospital at Amonate is shown in this 1942 photograph. Because of the remote locations of the coalmines, the company had to provide the services and conveniences of modern life. (From the author's collection.)

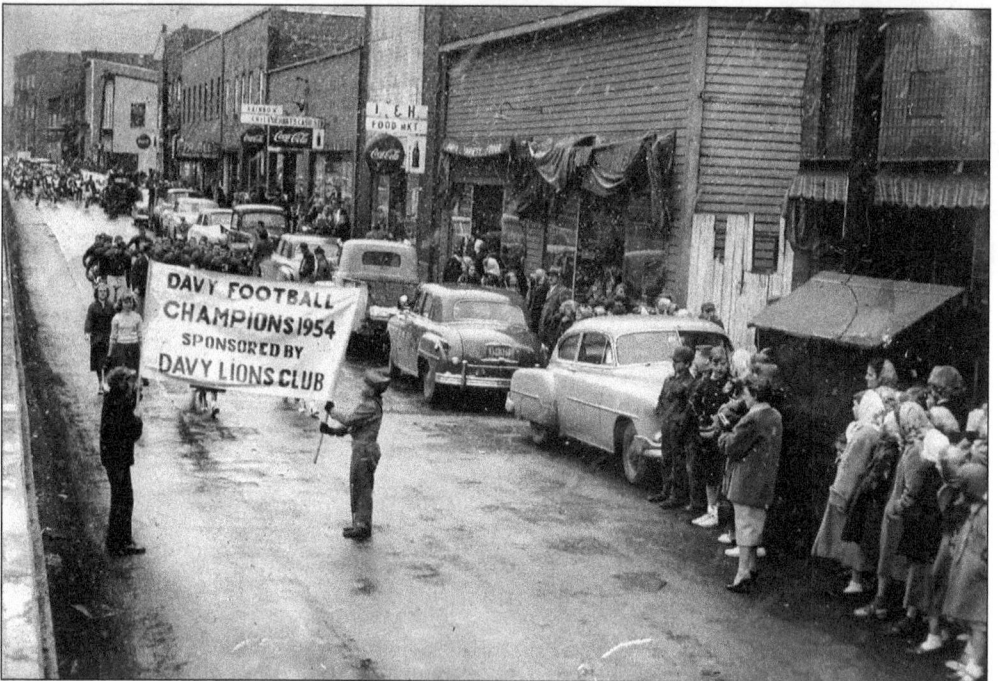

WELCOME CHAMPS. People lined the streets of Davy to welcome home the 1954 championship football team. High school sports continue to play a major role in the community. (Courtesy of Ron Dalton.)

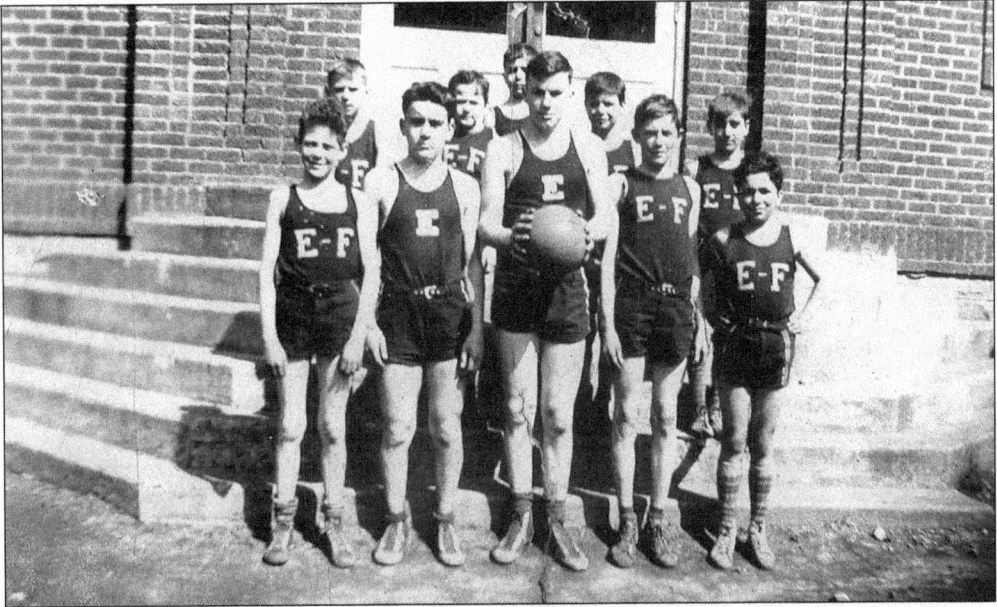

ROUND BALL. Members of the Elbert-Filbert Elementary School basketball team shown in this 1937 photo are, from left to right, (front row) Steve Colosi, Ed Shauffer, Mario Defelice, Lewis Defelice, and George Davis; (back row) Harry Filie, Albert Lopez, Carlo Columbo, Steve Blasher, and John Gregory. (Courtesy of Patricia Kadar.)

HOOP DREAMS. The Gary District Bulldogs won five out of six regional titles in the Colored Sectional Tournament from 1935 through 1941, winning the state championship in the final year before World War II. Lewis Johnson was the top scorer of the tournament, but three others—Latham Ross, James Shelton, and Hariston Padgett—joined him in the top ten. Legendary coach ? Wilkerson is at the far left. (Courtesy of Sam Johnson.)

WORKERS OF THE WORLD. Students in the Gary High School manual training class are shown in this March 9, 1925 photograph. The only student identified is Abbie Whitney Hunt, at right with the broad white collar. (Courtesy of Patricia Kadar.)

MAN IN THE KNOW. The incomparable Mike Hornick, shown above at right with the author, assembled an incredible collection of coalfield artifacts and photographs in order to tell the story of McDowell County. (Photo by Phil Farmer.)

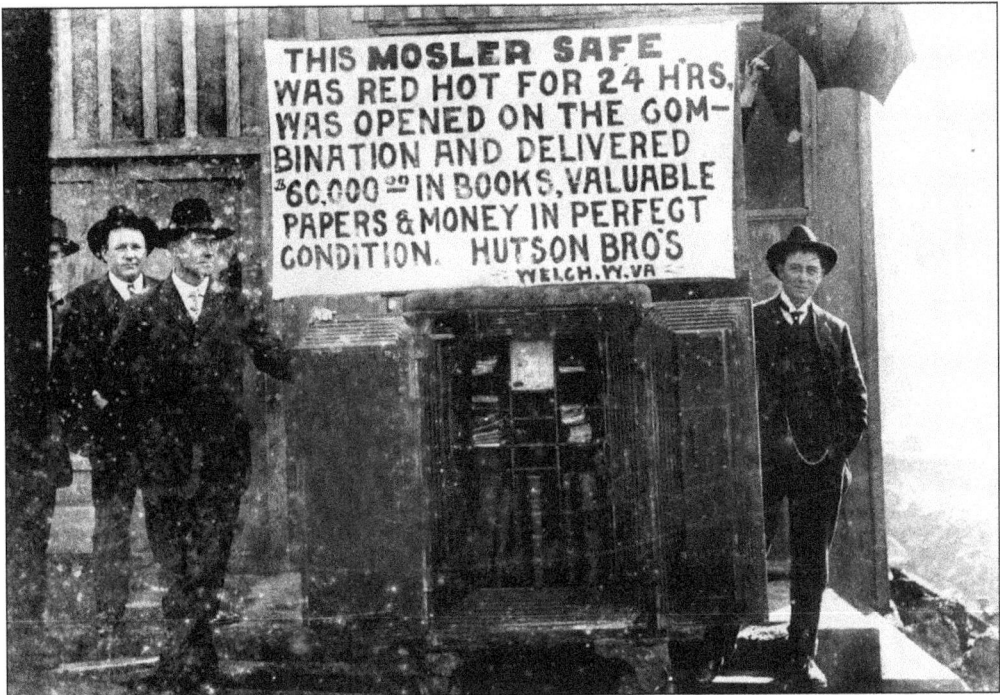

NOW THAT'S SAFE. Some unidentified promoters are shown here extolling the virtues of the Mosler Safe in this early 20th-century photograph. (Courtesy of Rose Marino.)

BIKER. An unknown unicyclist is shown here, apparently taking a bow after demonstrating his ability on the contraption. The actual location of the photo is unknown, but it is believed to have been taken somewhere in the Elkhorn Bottom section. (Courtesy of Lindsay Grubb.)

ACTIVIST. Suzanne Slaughter is shown here at a McDowell County Museum Commission meeting. Slaughter and others leaders of the county's African-American community worked tirelessly to restore the Kimball War Memorial. (Photo by the author.)

MEETING PLACE. After its dedication in 1928, the Kimball War Memorial, dedicated to black veterans of World War I, served as a meeting place for the community. The memorial is believed to be the only one of its kind in the United States. (From the author's collection.)

WINNER. Jennings Boyd coached the Northfork Blue Demons basketball team for 15 seasons, and during that time, he set a national record for state basketball championships with eight straight from 1974 to 1981. He died April 2, 2002. (*Bluefield Daily Telegraph* archives.)

DOC. Dr. L.L. Whitney is shown here making a house call. Whitney served as company physician during the 1920s for U.S. Coal and Coke in Gary. (Courtesy of Patricia Kadar.)

SIMPLY RED. Ernest "Red" Carroll is shown here with Dr. Les Hollon, pastor of St. Matthew's Baptist Church in Louisville, Kentucky, one of a steady stream of people who have made their way to Coalwood to visit the home of the "Rocket Boys." Carroll's son, Jimmy (O'Dell) Carroll, was one of Homer Hickam's Rocket Boys, but Red played a nurturing role for all of the young men. He continues to guide tours through the community to share images of places mentioned in the book and the movie *October Sky*. (Photo by the author.)

Five

COMMUNITIES

ALL SMILES. Students of Welch School gathered outside the building to pose for this "100 Percent Clean Teeth & Healthy Mouths" activity. The county went from just a few thousand people in 1880 to tens of thousands by the first decade of the 20th century. (Courtesy of Rose Marino.)

ONE BUSY DOWNTOWN. According to some sources, the scene outside the Pocahontas Theater on McDowell Street in downtown Welch prompted the editors of the *Saturday Evening Post* to use this 1947 photograph to illustrate a story about a fictional town in Indiana. Although stories about the photo abound, there is no question that it is downtown Welch. (Courtesy of Louise Warden.)

YOU'LL NEVER GET RICH. Appalachian Power Company workers in downtown Welch are shown in 1925 installing power lines below the surface of the street in an innovative construction project. In spite of its mountainous, rural location, the city of Welch has a rich tradition of coming up with unique ways to address new challenges. (Courtesy of Rose Marino.)

CITY ON THE TUG. Welch was incorporated in 1893 and named for surveyor I.A. Welch, who founded the city. The city experienced dramatic growth after this 1903 photograph. (Courtesy of Grubb Photo Service.)

ANOTHER VIEW. Welch became the McDowell County seat in 1892, prior to the city's incorporation. Fueled by the booming timber and coal industry, the village grew into a mighty city within a decade. (Courtesy of Grubb Photo Service.)

MORE WELCH. As the city began to grow, Welch took on an appearance all its own. With just a narrow strip of bottomland to build on, residents and businesses slowly moved up the mountains to carve building sites out of stone. (Courtesy of Rose Marino.)

FILL HER UP WITH ETHYL. The old Three-Way Filling Station in Welch, at the intersection of Wyoming and McDowell Streets, was a popular stop for motorists in the early days of the city. (Courtesy of Rose Marino.)

ON SOLID GROUND. The McDowell County National Bank (MCNB) has served the city, county, and surrounding communities for many years from the same location on Wyoming Street in Welch. (Courtesy of Rose Marino.)

INSIDE JOB. It is income tax day for these unidentified bank personnel, inside what some believe to be the MCNB. The bank has had a highly successful run and has recently opened up a new location in Princeton. (Courtesy of Rose Marino.)

STAMPS OF APPROVAL. In response to the incredible growth throughout the coalfields, the U.S. Post Office attempted to have employees sort mail on buses as they weaved through the mountainous roads. James Vaiden, at left inside the bus, said it was a challenging experience—especially for his tummy. (Courtesy of James Vaiden.)

BANK OPENS. McDowell County Bank opened July 1, 1900, with I.J. Rhodes, R.W. Nickell, Warren Wilson, and Roscoe McClure on the job. (Courtesy of Grubb Photo Service.)

WELCH LOVES A PARADE. Hundreds of people pack McDowell Street each November 11 to watch the units participating in the annual Veterans Day parade, like this one in 1970. The Welch 40 and 8 and American Legion Post 8 launched the tradition of honoring veterans on November 11 in 1919. Prominent speakers at the event have included presidents Harry Truman and Lyndon Johnson. The 40 and 8 is an organization within the American Legion so named because French boxcars headed to the battlefront could carry 40 men and 8 mules. (Courtesy of Rose Marino.)

SAME PLACE, DIFFERENT YEAR. The photo above shows another Veterans Day parade sometime later in the 1970s but roughly from the same location. In addition to the parade, the American Legion post hosts a dinner in honor of the speaker on the night before the parade. (Courtesy of Nick Mason.)

A PLACE OF HEALTHCARE. By 1948, Welch Emergency Hospital (now Welch Community Hospital) had established several specialties to help coalminers and their families with injuries and illnesses peculiar to the industry and region. (Courtesy of Robert Presley Jr.)

SECOND OPINION. Welch and McDowell County residents could also seek help for their medical maladies at the physician-owned Grace Hospital on Virginia Avenue in Welch. Dr. Charles Hicks opened Grace Hospital on February 25, 1923. (Courtesy of Robert Presley Jr.)

FROM A FIRE. Firefighters with the first Welch Fire Department are shown here in this 1919 photograph. The department boasted two reels of hose. Dr. Dewey Mitchell is seated in the front bumper; Reece Helmandollar is on the hood; John Blakely is at the right of the driver's seat; and Felix Barley is on the seat at the rear. (Courtesy of Grubb Photo Service.)

BANK BLUES. The old First National Bank of Welch was one of several banks in McDowell County that did not survive the Great Depression. The bank was organized April 1, 1902, as the Citizens Bank of Welch but converted to the national banking system in 1908. It was placed on voluntary liquidation on June 30, 1930, and some of its assets were taken over by McDowell County National Bank. (Courtesy of Grubb Photo Service.)

COURTHOUSE. The McDowell County Courthouse in Welch is among the stateliest seats of county government in West Virginia. The first county seat met August 23, 1858, in what is now English, but it was moved to Welch in 1895, although the physical building was not completed until about the turn of the 20th century. (Courtesy of Grubb Photo Service.)

ROAD WORK. Construction of the U.S. Route 52 Bypass is shown here in front of the Stevens Clinic in the mid-1940s. A two-mile stretch of Route 52 from Lake Superior to Big Four opened on July 1, 1944. (Courtesy of Rose Marino.)

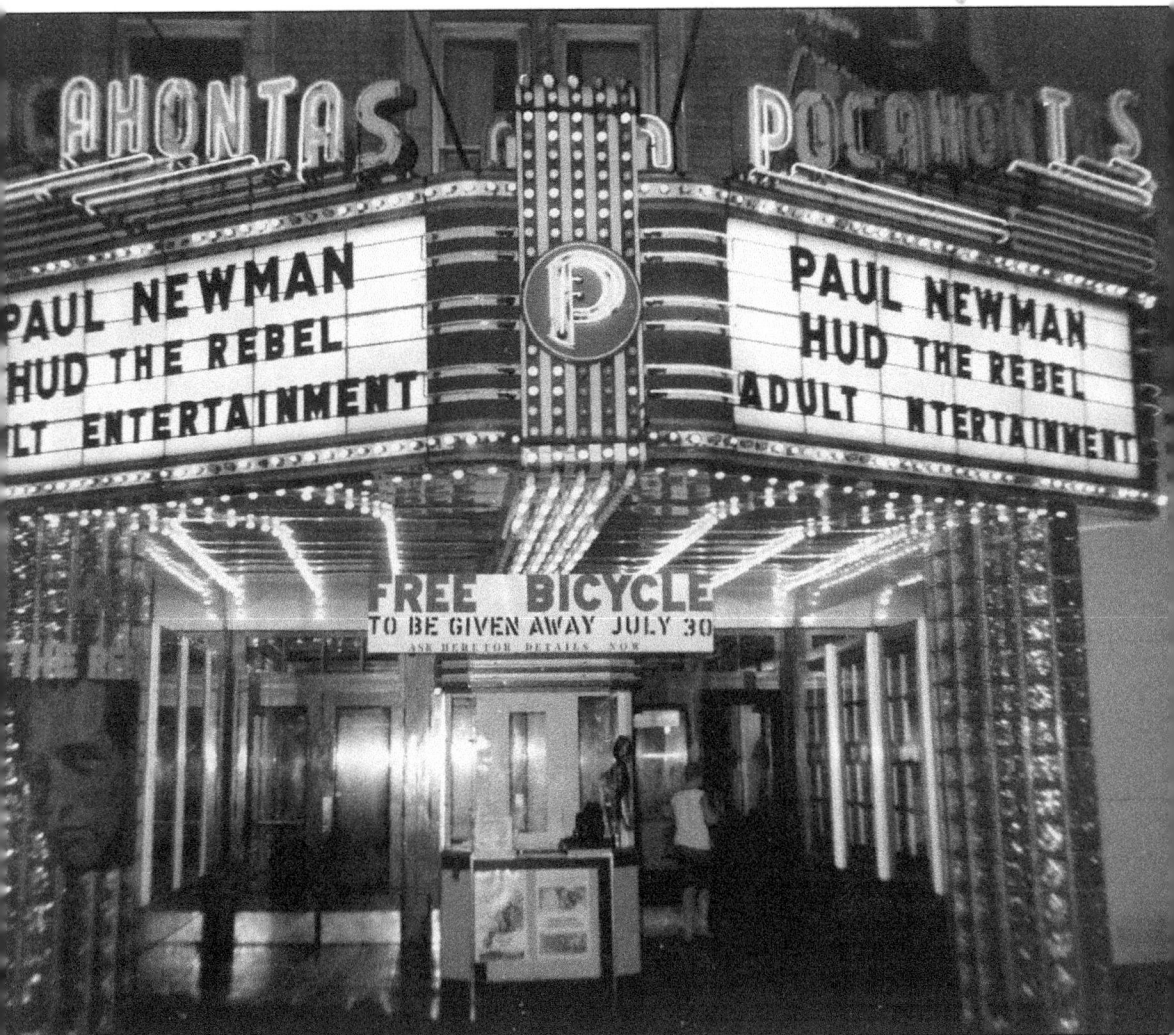

THE BIG PICTURE. The Pocahontas Theater on McDowell Street in downtown Welch gave people from throughout the coalfields a way to escape through entertainment. The theater is shown here in the summer of 1963, at a time when a motion picture like *Hud* would be considered adult entertainment. (Photo by Jim Cristea.)

HOMEGROWN GENERAL. Lt. Gen. Robert E. Gray served as keynote speaker at the Welch 40 and 8 Veterans Day Parade on November 11, 2004. Gray was born in Algoma and is one of five generals born in McDowell County. (Photo by the author.)

TRIBUTE REMEMBERED. Members of Welch 40 and 8 resurrected this relic of the past from an open field in South Charleston, restored it, and put it in a place of honor near Coney Island in Welch. After World War I, the people of France decorated 49 boxcars—one for each state and the District of Columbia—and filled them with gifts of appreciation for the American people. (Photo by the author.)

MEMORIAL RECALLED. The southern West Virginia coalfields was a bustling place when the United States declared war on Germany in 1916, and hundreds of young men volunteered to serve their nation. When they returned home, they worked with the county commission to build the nation's first World War Memorial Building. The building was completed in 1920 but is no longer standing. (Courtesy of Tim Hairston.)

MEMORIAL FOR BLACK DOUGH BOYS. During segregation, blacks and whites could not use the same facilities, but the many African-American soldiers from McDowell County sought to remember the service of their comrades. Working with the county commission, the black soldiers erected the nation's first War Memorial to honor black veterans of World War I. The building is located in Kimball and has recently been restored. (From the author's collection.)

105

A NEW NATION. On November 12, 1788, Henry Harman and two of his sons, George and Matthias, engaged a group of seven Black Wolf Indians of the Shawnee Tribe at a point on the Tug Fork of the Big Sandy River near a community now known as Black Wolf. The Harman family prevailed in the battle. This stone was erected at the site of the battle in 1927 but was moved to the Gary Lions Park in the 1990s. (Courtesy of Grubb Photo Service.)

ROAD SHOW. This scene of Maybeury, looking east toward Bramwell on August 22, 1951, shows the dramatic double-track Norfolk Southern Railway trestle, in continuous use since its construction. (From the author's collection.)

CLARK SECTION. The town of Northfork was originally known as Clark, but as the community grew, the name Northfork became standard because of the community's location where the North Fork of Elkhorn Creek intersects with the main creek. (Courtesy of Grubb Photo Service.)

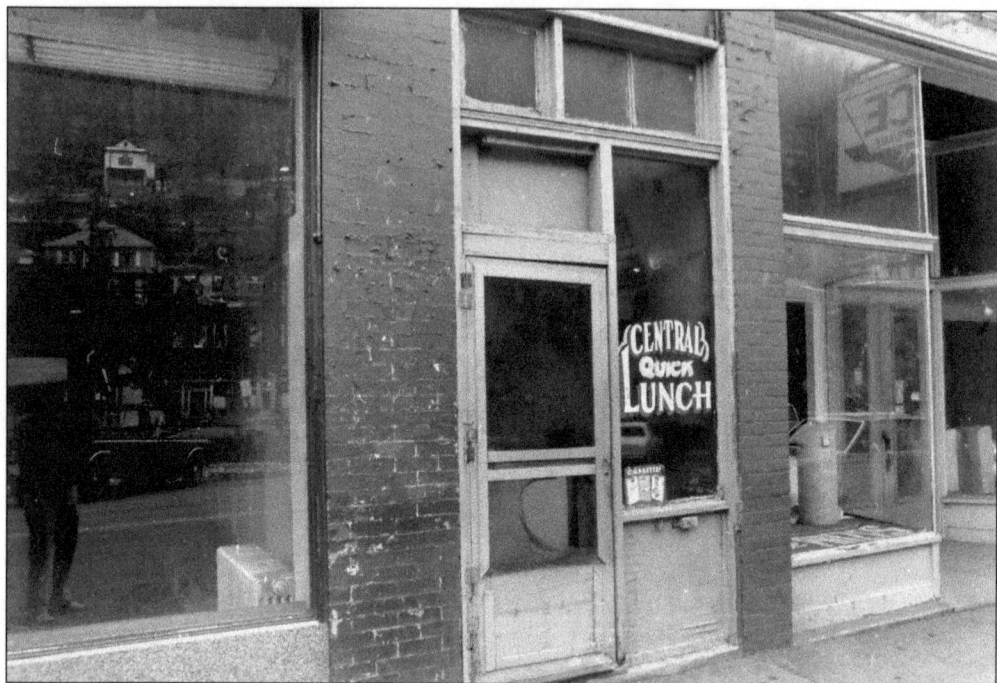

HOLE IN THE WALL. One of Northfork's most unique restaurants was the Central Quick Lunch, located on U.S. Route 52 in the heart of the main business section of the community. The restaurant was 70 inches wide and 90 feet long. (Photo by Phil Farmer.)

INSIDE THE CENTRAL. James Kemp, the cook at Central Quick Lunch (at right, talking to the author) boasted of serving the best liver sandwiches in the state of West Virginia. Of the restaurant's unusual dimensions, he said only that if a six-foot-tall man fell down, "he'd be in trouble." (Photo by Phil Farmer.)

ACROSS TOWN. The town of Northfork is split down the middle by U.S. Route 52, Elkhorn Creek, and the Norfolk Southern mainline. The above photo shows the main business section of the city on the east side of the tracks. (Courtesy of Rose Marino.)

MOVIE HOUSE. The old Freeman Theater in Northfork was a popular place for local residents to come and enjoy the best of what Hollywood had to offer. (Courtesy of Rose Marino.)

BUSES. The old bus terminal in War gave people a chance to make connections to the outside world. Although he had long since moved on, Jack Craft, who built his Consolidated Bus Lines into an empire, got his start in the late 1920s in War. One of the region's most tragic school-bus accidents occurred near War on October 12, 1939, killing seven students. (Courtesy of Robert Presley Jr.)

POP SHOP. The Old Bearre's Garage in Davy was a popular spot, as evidenced by this 1938 photograph. (Courtesy of Louise Warden.)

HEART OF TOWN. Downtown Iaeger was a busy place, as can be seen in this vintage photograph. The community was originally best known for the timber industry it supported, but it soon grew in prominence as a railhead for the coal industry. (Courtesy of Rose Marino.)

BIG BEND IN THE TUG. The state division of highways erected a massive bridge over the Tug Fork and Norfolk Southern mainline to carry travelers on U.S. Route 52 in the mid-1990s. The river flows around Johnny Cake Mountain. (Aerial photo by Mel Grubb.)

FAITH OF OUR FATHERS. The old St. Mary's Russian Orthodox Church, located in the Crozer Bottom section of Elkhorn, always appeared somewhat enigmatic when viewed by visitors to the county traveling on U.S. Route 52. The church's gold-colored belfry had a decidedly different look from the other churches of the region. Coalminers of all faiths came to work in the southern West Virginia coalfields, and while the congregation of St. Mary's has moved to Bluefield, the old church remains as a reminder of the region's rich heritage. (Photo by Evonda Archer.)

PLACE OF WORSHIP. The Marytown Community Church was built *c.* 1923, during the time when the community experienced resurgence thanks to famed automaker Henry Ford acquiring coal properties in the Marytown area. He was considering resourceful ways of getting his coal to steel mills near his automobile plants in Detroit. (Courtesy of Rose Marino)

BANK ON IT. The First National Bank of Keystone (center), Keystone Hardware (right), the JLT Convenience Store/Carwash (foreground left), and the Pig Pen motorcycle shop (center foreground) all represented parts of the financial empire owned and operated by Terry L. Church, senior vice-president of the bank, who received a long federal prison sentence on fraud and obstruction charges. (Aerial photo by Mel Grubb.)

AUDITORS GO HOME. Bank examiners with the FDIC and the Office of the Comptroller of the Currency arrived in vans on September 1, 1999, to start the process of unraveling the massive fraud that led to the collapse of the bank. A person or persons unknown spray-painted "Auditors Go Home" on a building near the bank while the 1999 examination was underway. (Photo by the author.)

114

MANSION ON THE HILL. Billie Jean Cherry, chairman of the First National Bank of Keystone, purchased the James Ellwood Jones mansion in Switchback at auction, after it had been the site of a Valentine's Day 1998 triple homicide. Jones was vice president and superintendent of Pocahontas Fuel in the early 1900s, until his death at the mansion on November 25, 1932. (Aerial photo by Mel Grubb.)

ROOM TO MOVE. Jones imported 66 stained-glass windows from Scotland for this room, which featured hardwood floors and a mahogany ceiling. Jones was a supporter of good roads and good schools in McDowell County. He invented several machines to improve coal mining and provided numerous college scholarships to students of McDowell and Mercer Counties. He died in this room while playing cards with Dr. I.C. Peters. (Photo by the author.)

ON TOP OF THE WORLD. Terry Lee Church dumped millions of ill-gotten gains she pilfered from the First National Bank of Keystone into her compound on top of Burke Mountain, C & H Ranch. Several of Church's family members lived in residences in the compound. On July 18, 1999, Church instructed employees to dig a trench 150 feet long, 10 feet wide, and 10 feet deep at a place called "Cat House Field" (top of photo), where she instructed them to bury vital bank records, computer files, and other materials related to the massive fraud at the bank. The losses at Keystone cost the FDIC Insurance Fund over $750 million, making it one of the top 10 bank failures since the FDIC was established in 1933. (Aerial photo by Mel Grubb.)

Six

FLOODS

UNDERWATER. On July 8, 2001, a flash flood ripped through several McDowell County communities, severely damaging homes and property, like this house in Shawnee Bottom near Landgraff. (Photo by the author.)

FLASH FLOOD WARNING. Flash floods in McDowell County are not a new development. The steep mountain slopes, which have been timbered and mined for years, send water rushing into narrow valleys, where the only suitable building sites are located, as this *c.* 1910 photo can attest. (Courtesy of H.C. "Kit" Lewis Jr.)

RAGING WATERS. Floodwaters ripped through the Northfork Hollow community of Gilliam Bottom on July 8, 2001. Local residents believe the loss of life was minimized because the flooding occurred around noon on a Sunday, when most county residents were in church. (Photo by Tim Hairston.)

FLOOD AFTERMATH. Residents of the Norwood addition of Kimball dragged tons of personal belongings out of their flood-ravaged homes after the July 8, 2001 flood. (Photo by Tim Hairston.)

FOR WHAT IT'S WORTH. The Northfork Hollow community of Worth was absolutely ravaged by floodwaters and debris related to the July 2001 flood. (Photo by Tim Hairston.)

HIGH WATER MARK. Devastating floods on July 8, 2001, and 10 months later on May 2, 2002, seemed to dominate everything about life in the county. Another flood on November 22, 2003, caused some problems in the county, but an aggressive streambed restoration project prevented any serious problems. (Photo by the author.)

CALL OUT THE GUARD. Former governor Bob Wise (in front seat) is shown here with McDowell County Emergency Services director Jimmy Joe Gianato as they tour flood-damaged areas in the county following the 2001 flood. (Photo by the author.)

QUAGMIRE. Virginia Avenue in Welch did not even resemble a city street a day after the May 2, 2002 flood. While the flood 10 months earlier was spread throughout southern West Virginia, its companion flood seemed to concentrate its power on McDowell County and neighboring Buchanan County, Virginia. County communications were cut off for a time when the 911 Center flooded. Several areas that were untouched in the 2001 flood were slammed in 2002. Seven people lost their lives in the 2002 flood. (Photo by Tim Hairston.)

PREMIER. Flash flooding hammered away at residences and businesses on the Northwest side of Premier Mountain, as this picture taken two days after the May 2, 2002 flood will attest. (Photo by Evonda Archer.)

UNEXPECTED FLOOD WATERS. Residents living on the Welch side of Coalwood saw the normally sleepy stream near their homes transformed into a raging torrent in the May 2, 2002 flood. (Photo by Evonda Archer.)

THE RAIL THING. Norfolk Southern track repair crews had their hands full trying to restore mainline service through communities like Kimball after water covered the tracks during the flood on May 2, 2002. (Photo by Tim Hairston.)

CONVOY AHEAD. Soldiers with National Guard units based in West Virginia, Virginia, Tennessee, Kentucky, Ohio, Pennsylvania, and South Carolina answered the call to restore order to the communities ravaged by both floods. Guardsmen are shown working in Kimball after the 2001 flood. (Photo by the author.)

FAITH-BASED RESPONSE. Various faith-based organizations from throughout the United States came to McDowell County to help people clear their homes of flood-damaged debris and clean tons of mud out of basements and living areas. Some organizations, like Minnesota-based YouthWorks, were already on the scene when the July 2001 flood hit, but other groups of young people and adults arrived after word of the floods spread. (Photo by Tim Hairston.)

Shattered Dreams. This haunting image of a baby doll's head lying in the remnants of a Coalwood asphalt road washed away in the May 2, 2002 flood underscores the massive loss of personal property that accompanied each flood. (Photo by Evonda Archer.)

On Guard. Soldiers with the South Carolina National Guard are shown here receiving expressions of gratitude from West Virginia secretary of safety Joe Martin following their service during the 2001 flood. (Photo by the author.)

HE'D RATHER BE RACING. Lt. Jamie Fowler of Alpha Company, 122nd Engineering Battalion, South Carolina National Guard, devoted six weeks of his time and energy in 2001 to restore order to flood-ravaged McDowell County. Fowler is from Darlington, South Carolina, home of the Superspeedway. (Photo by the author.)

ALL SMILES. Pfc. ? Casterline is shown here between two southern West Virginia beauties, Denise Nicole Lewis (left) of Lewisburg, 2001 Miss Four Seasons Country, and Allison Spadaro (right) of Princeton, 2001 Miss Mercer County, at a USO-style show in August 2001 at Mount View High School, held to thank soldiers of the National Guard. (Photo by the author.)

WORK ZONE. Landgraff was particularly hard hit by the July 2001 flood and the May 2, 2002 flood. Since the time of the second flood, state officials, under the watchful eyes of federal authorities, completed a countywide stream-channel restoration project that cleared blocked areas from streams and provided peace of mind for people still living in the vicinity of McDowell County's mountain streams. (Photo by Tim Hairston.)

ADVENTURES AWAIT. The author is shown here in June 1991 pointing to the "hole in the wall" that serves traffic between Marytown and Davy. The tunnel was likely built for a long-forgotten railroad line between the two communities. Even though the roof is unsupported and the walls are jagged, the old tunnel gets plenty of use. Many unusual, unique, and interesting sights await visitors to the Free State of McDowell. (Photo by Evonda Archer.)

www.ingramcontent.com/pod-product-compliance
Lightning Source LLC
Chambersburg PA
CBHW050654110426

42813CB00007B/2012